GIVEN IN LOVE

For mothers who are choosing an adoption plan

By Maureen Connelly

Design by Janet Sieff, Centering Corporation

ISBN: 978-1-56123-010-5

Centering Corporation
Omaha, NE 68104

1-866-218-0101
1-402-553-1200

www.centering.org

ABOUT THIS BOOK

Choosing an adoption plan is one of the most difficult decisions you will ever have to make.

The mother who releases her baby is not usually recognized as a grieving mother.

Because you made this decision, people assume you do not feel sad or have a sense of loss.

This book has been lovingly written to help you prepare for the separation and loss of your child, and to support you during the grief that you may experience.

MONTHS OF WAITING

During the past few months you have had many emotions.
You've probably been scared, hurt, angry, sad, hopeful and
proud – all at the same time. You've found out which friends
were real and supportive, and there have been times when you
had to do things alone.

You've done a lot of thinking. This is one of the most difficult
decisions of your life – choosing an adoption plan. You've
probably done a lot of talking to family and friends, counselors
and medical people.

Now your pregnancy is over. The waiting is finished. It's time to
let your baby go. But first, there are even more things to consider.

MORE DECISIONS

Right after the birth of your baby, you will once again be faced
with important decisions:

- Do you want to see your baby?
- Do you want to hold your baby?
- Do you want to name your baby?
- Would you like pictures taken of your baby?
- Do you want any mementos such as the baby's hospital braclet,
  lock of hair, footprints, handprints, or birth certificate?

Before saying "No," give yourself some time to think about
what you really want to do and then make your decisions. Some
people think that seeing your baby will make you sad. Some
think you will change your mind or question your decision.
Some people think that avoiding grief makes it go away.
Unfortunately, that's usually not the case. Most women find it
easier to say "Goodbye" if they first say "Hello."

Another reason to see the baby is to answer any questions you may have about your baby's looks and health. This can be especially valuable if you have other children in the future. If that time comes, you won't wonder about how this baby looked or if he or she was healthy.

Some mothers who don't see their babies at all, or for just a few minutes in the delivery room, can have a sense of unfinished work, or they may feel they have done a lot of work for nothing.

Remember, you are in control of your decisions. You are the one who decides whether or not to see your baby.

Seeing, Touching, Holding –
IF YOU DECIDE TO SAY "HELLO"

As painful as it may seem to see your baby, this may be the only time you have together after your baby's birth. For the past nine months, you held your baby under your heart. Now you can hold your baby to your heart.

It is important for you to touch, feel, examine, and know everything you can about this baby. What is the baby's

> Weight?
> Length?
> Eye Color?
> Hair?

These memories will become lifelong treasures never to be forgotten. Take as much time as you need. You may want to write things down so you can remember them. There is a section in the back of this book for doing that.

PICTURES AND MEMENTOS

When you are separated from someone you love, the best way to remember that person is through pictures. Pictures can be a real source of comfort to you both now and in the future.

If you don't have a camera, ask a nurse if she can take pictures. Nurseries usually have a Polaroid or other type of camera handy.

My mother thought I was crazy when I called and told her to bring her camera to the hospital and take pictures. She said it would only make me feel worse. Well, she was wrong. At first, I looked at the pictures several times a day, but now, a year later, I just get them out on Robbie's birthday. I'm really glad I have them.

It's also the time to have a picture taken of any staff person who was helpful and supportive of you. Again, taking pictures is something that must be decided now. This will be your only chance.

If the nursery doesn't offer you objects to help you remember your baby and your time together, ask for them.

You might ask for the crib card, bracelet, tape measure, blanket, footprints, hand prints, and a lock of hair, if your baby has hair.

Finally, ask a nurse if there is anything more she would suggest you take home. Nurseries use different things and your nurse may have additional ideas for mementos.

Crib Card
Bracelet
Tape Measure
Blanket
Footprints
Hand Prints
Lock of Hair

NAMING YOUR BABY

You may not have thought about giving your baby a name. Some birth mothers feel they don't have the right or need to choose a name, since the name the adoptive parents choose is likely to be different.

We disagree. We think naming your baby can be important. It will give your baby an identity. A name will reflect the special bond between you and your baby. You can talk about your baby by name and know you are talking about a real person. Most birth moms say this name becomes very special and important.

I hadn't thought about naming my baby. I guess I figured that if I wasn't going to know her, I didn't need to give her a name. But when the nurse asked me if I was going to name her, I thought about it and named her after me. After all, she'd been an important part of me.

NO "IF ONLYS"

Seeing, touching, holding your baby and saying goodbye takes care of one other thing. You won't, in the future, wish you had done all these things. You won't sit someday and say, "If only I had…"

If Onlys are painful. Many of them can't be undone. You don't need more stress and grief in the future when you can take care of finishing your business with your baby right now.

6

SAYING GOODBYE

It may be helpful to actually say "Goodbye" out loud while holding your baby, or whenever you choose to say it. It's okay to cry with your baby and let your child hear your voice and good wishes for the future. Along with verbally saying goodbye to their babies, many birth mothers have found it comforting and helpful to write a letter to their child.

When you write a letter, you express your love for your child and the reasons and circumstances for choosing an adoption plan. Try to provide as much information as you can about your child's family and heritage and give information about the birth father.

We all need to know our roots. A letter from you can answer a lot of questions from your child in the years to come.

Many birth mothers also write letters to the couple who will become your baby's parents. If you do this, you acknowledge your love and feelings for your baby and the reasons for choosing an adoption plan. If you know some of your medical history and the medical history of your family, it's a good idea to include that, too.

YOUR LETTER

If you write a letter, your child will know of your love, that your decision for choosing an adoption plan was made out of love, not out of not wanting your child. Your letter is also a way of sharing your good wishes for your child. It is likely to be the only message of love your child will ever have from you, and it will be very valuable.

I started writing, and at first I wanted everything to be perfect, like I was doing it for an English teacher. Then I thought how stupid that was. This would be some little piece of me that my baby could love and have for as long as he lived, so I just pretended I was sitting there talking to him when he was about 10 years old.

Here are two letters so you can see what we mean.

My Dearest Nicole:

First, I want you to know how much I love you! You have the parents you have because they love you with all their hearts and want the best for you, too. I was not married when you were born. I was afraid you would be put down and talked about. I know my family thought I had done a very bad thing getting pregnant, but that wasn't your fault. You were a perfect baby before you were born and after you were born, and now I know you are a very special girl.

I had a lot to say about picking the people who became your parents. Everyone, me… the social service people who worked with me… and your parents, wanted only good for you. I love you enough to give you the best home I can. I hope that you will one day understand why we can't be together. I think of you often. I know you have a good family. I see in your parents a love that goes way beyond the average couple. You are part of a whole family now, and so many people love you. Always remember, you were very much wanted. By everyone!

Finally, I want you to know one thing, Nicole. Your mother and father are your real parents. They are raising you and guiding you through life. They have been through trials and good times with you. They have provided for your needs and given you love and support. They would move heaven and earth to help you. They chose you and I am grateful.

I carried you for nine months and gave birth to you. During that nine months I talked with you while you were in my womb. I loved you. You and I have a bond that no one can take away, nor time nor circumstance can change it. I will always love you, Nicki, and carry a part of you with me. Please take care of yourself and let your family be a source of help and comfort and let God be the mainstay in your life.

Love,
Your Birth Mother

8

To Landon's New Parents,

I want you to know right off that I really care about this baby. I didn't mean to get pregnant, and I can't keep him. I don't have the money and I don't have a job. Some of my friends have kept their babies, and it didn't work out. I can tell that they aren't happy and like one of them said, she saw a poster that said having a baby is like being grounded for 18 years. I wouldn't mind being grounded if I could give Landon what he needs. I can't for a long time.

I know you can give him those things. You can give him a mother and a father. You can give him good things and an education. I know you really, really want him and that he'll be very loved. Always let him know that I chose an adoption plan because I love him, too, and I know this is best for him.

I named him Landon. It's not a family name, just one I liked. I know you'll find a name you like, too. I don't plan on ever seeing Landon again, but if he wants to meet me when he's old enough, I'll be happy to see him and talk to him.

Please take good care of him. Love him like you've never loved a baby before. He's all yours, but he's also a part of me.

I'm sending my family's medical history and some of the medical history of the father's family, too.

Thank you,

Landon's Birth Mother

GRIEF AND LETTING GO

To remember is painful.
To forget is impossible.

Whenever we lose or let go of something or someone precious, we experience grief. When you choose an adoption plan, you're very likely to be sad for a while and have some, if not all, the feelings a mother has when a baby dies. You may be surprised to find that the separation and loss of your baby is very physically and emotionally painful.

You may find you have a strange combination of grief and relief. You may feel grief over the loss of your baby and relief that your decision has been made, your pregnancy completed, and your life can get back on line. It's important to know that the feelings you are experiencing are normal. Even though you know in your heart that you made the right decision to choose an adoption plan, you still hurt, and hurting is okay. Grief is a part of everyone's life.

Grief comes in many forms. Some of it is physical, some of it is emotional or psychological, and some can be spiritual.

PHYSICAL GRIEF

I was so tired all the time! I thought all I wanted to do was get out of the hospital, start exercising and get my life back to normal. But I couldn't sleep, I ate everything in the refrigerator, and once when I saw a sad movie, I broke down into tears.

Just as you grieve emotionally, your body grieves, too. You may:
• Cry often and at unexpected times
• Experience a tight feeling in your throat
• Have a heavy sensation in your chest
• Have no appetite or want to eat all the time
• Have difficulty sleeping, or want to sleep too much
• Dream of your baby or have frightening dreams

Remember that your body is not only grieving, it is also working hard to return to an un-pregnant state. You have a lot of hormone changes, weight changes, and general body work happening. It's more important now than ever before to take good care of yourself.

Eat Good Foods
Now is the time for lots of vegetables, fruit, skim milk and healthy foods that give you energy. Your nurse can give you a list of foods that are good for you and will help you recover. If you're usually over-weight, now is the time to start trimming up with really good healthy food. It can make a difference for the rest of your life.

Exercise
Exercise is a good way to handle grief and get your shape back at the same time. Your nurses will have some after-baby exercises you can do. Later on you can do more, like walking, swimming, or dancing.

Your Follow-up Check-Up
About six weeks after your baby is born, you need to see your doctor to make sure your body is getting back to normal. This check-up is really important. During this six weeks, listen to your body. Call right away if you have any pain, heavy bleeding, a strange-smelling discharge from your vagina, burning pain when you go to the bathroom, or any fever.

Eat Good Foods

Exercise

Your Follow-up Check-up

PSYCHOLOGICAL GRIEF

This is the emotional pull that grief has on us. Some of these feelings are due to adjusting hormones. Some occur because you're releasing your baby. Some feelings are just because of all the changes you are going through in your life right now.

• You may feel sad and depressed
• You're likely to be forgetful and act irritable
• Feel lonely or just plain numb and confused
• Be angry and have some unexplained anxiety
• Have trouble concentrating
• Feel detached
• Like the whole thing never happened
• Constantly think about the baby
• Feel guilty for choosing an adoption plan
• Feel guilty for having the baby and getting pregnant

GUILT

Of all aspects of grief, guilt is often the most troublesome. You can feel guilty about everything!

I felt awful! My family pretended nothing had happened. I felt guilty for letting the baby go, guilty for getting pregnant, and guilty because the father wouldn't talk to me. One day a friend complained about the weather and I realized I even felt guilty about rain! That was too much!

When you feel guilty, remember:
• You did what you could do with the knowledge, tools and circumstances you had at the time
• You finished your pregnancy and gave the world a new person
• You loved with the best kind of love
• You made sure your baby has a good chance in life

You are a good person!

GUILT AND ANGER

Guilt is unproductive behavior. If you need to ask someone to forgive you, then do it, either in person or a letter. If you need to forgive yourself, do it. You're worth it! Remember that everyone feels guilty at some time or another. It's what you do with it that's important. Now is the time to take care of your guilt and look ahead to your future.

Along with guilt, anger is one of the most difficult emotions that come with grief. You may feel angry:

• That you had to make this decision
• That circumstances were what they were
• At the birth father
• At your family
• At yourself
• At your doctor and staff
• At friends who deserted you
• At the couple who will get your baby
• At God

When you are angry, talk it out. Talk to someone who will listen without telling you what to think or feel. If you are working with a social worker, talk to her. Write it out. Keeping a journal is a good idea, and you can look back through it in six months and see how differently you feel.

I was mad at every little thing and I couldn't pin it down onto anything. I guess I was just mad that all this had happened to me.

Remember, feelings just are. They come suddenly and surprise you. While you can't always control your feelings, you can control what you do with them. When you are angry, hit the bed, walk, run, ride a bike or pound a pillow. One way to get rid of anger is to take a dish towel and hit your bed as hard as you can. It's okay to yell. It's okay to cry. Take it out in exercise or kitchen towels instead of taking it out on people or yourself.

SADNESS

There will probably be times when you need to let your tears flow. Crying is not breaking down, it's breaking into tears. Crying is a gentle melting. Don't hold your tears back if you need to cry. Don't be afraid that if you start to cry you won't stop.

You may have times when you think you're going crazy. Remember that feeling is normal, too. You've seen drastic and sudden changes in your life. You need time to adjust.

Time helps with grief. Gradually the pain lessens. You will begin to feel better.

This doesn't mean you forget. You can never forget important events in your life, and the last year has been a vital year for you. It's been a time of learning and experiencing and giving and grieving. You'll have more learning and growing and grieving in the year that is coming. Feel your feelings when you have them. Decide to grieve constructively. . .not by being bitter or angry, but by learning and growing.

Choosing an adoption plan is something you can go through and grow through.

THE OTHER PEOPLE IN YOUR LIFE

This was a time when I found out who my friends were. Some of my family surprised me, too. They were really there when I needed them. Others didn't care at all.

This is also a time when people don't quite know how to treat you. Whenever you have a major event or change or crisis in your life, you'll find that people become very cautious and careful around you. They don't know what to say and they don't want you to feel bad, so they usually don't say anything at all. It may seem as if they're pretending nothing really happened.

There will be a few members of your family and some friends with whom you can say anything. When you need to talk about yourself and your baby, find someone who will listen to you. Tell people how you feel. Tell your family and friends what you need.

Some young women feel they've let their families down. Keep in mind that every single person in the world feels like that at some time. Your family may be more worried about you than disappointed, more concerned than angry, and much more caring than you thought.

Again, tell someone how you feel, and if you are worried about how you're going to relate to each other in the future, talk to your social worker or your pastor or a counselor about getting all of you together for a session. It's something that would help almost all families now and then!

The Birth Father

If you and your baby's father still have a relationship, you probably decided together to release your baby. He, too, needs someone to talk to. Listen to each other.

Unfortunately, a lot of relationships that started out in love end in bitterness and anger. If you are alone now, you need to decide whether or not to let the father know about the baby. You may need to give medical and family history to your baby's new parents, and rightfully this should include both you and the father. You may need to ask the father for this information. However, everyone person is different and every situation is unique. If you're not sure what to do, talk to your social worker or counselor about this.

SPIRITUAL GRIEF

Earlier we listed the different kinds of grief – physical, emotional and spiritual. We've put the spiritual grief section here because we've also included a short service you can use for your baby if you wish.

Just as we grieve with our bodies and emotionally, we can grieve spiritually. When you grieve spiritually, you may:
• Have a lot of questions about God
• Feel God let you down
• Feel you let God down
• Ask, *Why Me?*

It's absolutely all right to have a lot of questions right now. If you have a spiritual leader who will listen without telling you what to think or feel, then talk with him or her. If there is a chaplain at your hospital, ask for a visit. Remember, you're a valuable person, and you deserve to have your questions and feelings answered by someone who cares.

I heard stuff about punishment and sin and I felt really bad. Then, I remembered an old poster I saw in church years ago. It said, "God doesn't make any junk." I decided this beautiful baby was far better than all the sin stuff. Giving her to a nice family was just as great a sacrifice for me as any listed in the Bible.

Some birth mothers have found it very helpful to have a special service for their baby.

We're including a sample service here. If you want, the hospital chaplain will help you with it. You can have your own spiritual leader, or you can just gather with family and friends. If you don't have a pastor or the hospital doesn't have a chaplain, ask nurses and social workers for the name of someone who would be good with this service and happy to do it for you. If you feel you don't want an actual service, then just read this quietly for yourself and your baby.

Song of your choice
To be played on cassette or CD, sung, played on guitar or other instrument.

Prayer
Great Creator – You who form us in your image, we thank you for your compassion and understanding in times of sadness and letting go. In the midst of our pains and joys, we gather today to give you thanks for this gift of new life. We thank you for this child's birth parent(s), who brought her/him into the world. At this time of letting go, we thank you for your presence which bonds us together in love.

Reflection by Chaplain or Clergy

Reflection by Birth mother
You do not have to do anything here. However, if you want, you can read your letter to your baby, read a poem, do what you want.

Blessing of the Child
(Chaplain/Clergy – holding the baby) Lord God, you who are mother and father to us, send forth your abundant blessing on this child who is made in your image. We pray this child will have the best home possible – one filled with faith, hope and deep love, a home and parents who will love as much as this child has been loved. Watch over and protect this child forever and ever.

Blessing of the Mother (or Parents)
(By Chaplain/Clergy) Dear God – I look to you at this turning point of my life as I place my beloved child for adoption. You, who knows the hearts of all creatures, know the pain I feel. Give me strength and courage, the strength to love and let go, the courage to live through the moments of doubt and sadness, knowing I made the best choice I could. God, bless my child. Help this child grow up healthy and happy. Guide this child in this life to know your ways. Help this child to know that out

there is always someone who loves him/her. Finally, You, the master of all life, help us realize that none of us own our children. Some are given the privilege of conceiving a child. Some are given the privilege of giving birth to this child. May I always be worthy of your love and your blessing.

Prayer for Adopting Parents (Everyone)

Bless the parents who will raise this child. Give them wisdom in their parenting. Help them love and protect this child. Even if we never meet, we share so much. We are partners in the creation of a human being. We thank you for their compassion and their caring. Give them strength and patience, gentleness and humor. We know they are excited now. We know they are as delighted as any expectant parents in the world. Soon they will have a day they will never forget – when this beautiful child comes home to them. Be with them as they guide and direct. Be present during sickness and anxiety. Be there, Lord, when they need you. We are privileged to be part of their love, God. We are honored to give this most precious of all gifts. Bless this couple and this family, Dear God.

Closing Response

We Remember Them

Chaplain/Clergy and all people present

In the rising of the sun and in its going down,
> **We remember them.**
In the blowing wind and the chill of winter,
> **We remember them.**
In the opening of buds and in the rebirth of spring,
> **We remember them.**
In the blue sky and warmth of summer,
> **We remember them.**
In the rustling of leaves and the beauty of autumn,
> **We remember them.**
In the beginning of the year when it ends,
> **We remember them.**

When we are weary and in need of strength,
We remember them.
When we have joys we yearn to share,
We remember them.
So long as we live, they too shall live, for they are now part of us as we remember them.

Final Blessing by Chaplain/Clergy

Our special thanks to the Seton Center in St. Paul, Minnesota, Rabbi Michael Gold and Rabbi Jack Reimer for prayers used in our service.

GETTING ON WITH YOUR LIFE

You've just had a baby, chosen an adoption plan, and are getting acquainted with the combination of pain, relief and grief. Now it's time to look to your future.

Time will help heal the pain you may feel now, both emotionally and physically. Not many women have gone through the experience you have just gone through. You have made a difficult decision and you've carried out plans you've made. You've thought through a lot of things and you've learned new ways to communicate and to live life. You will never forget your baby or what you have learned. All in all, what has happened to you can be one of the really big growth experiences of your life. You have a chance to look at how you've handled things, how you've matured and now how you cope with loss and letting go.

A few birth mothers have open adoptions where they visit their child and know how they are growing. Some birth mothers hope their child will contact them far in the future and they can get acquainted or they, themselves, try to make contact. Other birth mothers let go and never see or hear from their child again. No one can really tell right now which you will be. In each of these situations, there are good and bad results. In each there is pain to be faced.

Every major decision we make causes us to wonder about it in the future. There may be times when you wonder if you did the right thing. If that happens, remember how you feel right now and what the circumstances are and remember the gift you are giving to your baby. Letting go takes a lot of strength.

To love something
Is to let it go
To allow freedom
To grant space
To be not heavy clouds but gentle winds
To be not the fence but the open path
To be not the lock but the key,
For the greatest of embraces end with open arms
Permitting the ones loved to turn or return
As they wish.
This is love.

We wish you well as you begin your future.

The following pages are for you. They can be used to remember your baby.

THANK YOU FOR BEING YOU. . .

Baby's Name:
_____

Date of Birth:
_____

Place of Birth:
_____

Time of Birth:
_____

Baby's Weight:
_____

Baby's Length:
_____

Description of Hair:
_____

Special Features:
_____

Hospital:
_____

Doctor:
_____

Nurses:
_____

PHOTOGRAPHS, MEMENTOS, CERTIFICATES. . .

MY DREAMS AND WISHES FOR YOU...

ABOUT THE AUTHOR

Maureen Connelly went to college after the birth of her sixth child. Her first baby, Mary, died 10 minutes after she was born. Maureen has a Bachelor of Science Degree in Human Services from Fontbonne College, and is part of A.M.E.N.D. (Aiding Mothers & Fathers Experiencing Neonatal Death), where she counsels parents who have lost a baby. She is also a member of the bereavement program at Assumption Catholic Church. Maureen and her husband Tom live in St. Louis.

Special thanks to: Luke Leonard of Family Adoption & Counseling Services, St. Louis, Centering consultant Debra Chalpa, MeShell Lee of Adoption Center, Rabbi Gold, Rabbi Reimer, and the birth mothers who helped us.

ISBN: 1-56123-010-3
San: 298-1815

Centering Corporation
PO Box 4600
Omaha, NE 68104

Phone: 402-553-1200
Fax: 402-553-0507

Email: j1200@aol.com
Website: www.centering.org